Homographic Components in Homophonous Mandarin Characters Volume 2

by

Stephen M Kraemer

In looking at the graph-sound correspondence in modern Mandarin, many syllables in Mandarin are represented by more than one character. In a number of cases, however, although a certain Mandarin syllable is represented by more than one character, all the characters for this particular syllable share the same component, often a phonetic element. Such "homophonous" characters in Mandarin (different characters with the same syllable pronunciation) are represented by the same single “homographic” component. In general, the Mandarin writing system is considered quite irregular in its graph-sound correspondence, i.e., many syllables can be represented by more than one character, and a number of characters can have more than one pronunciation in Mandarin. However, examples of “homophonous” characters with a single “homographic” component exhibit a degree of regularity in the Mandarin system of graph-sound correspondence. In these cases, a particular Mandarin syllable may be represented by more than one character, but the same syllable is represented by only one repeating component.

In this study, homophonous Mandarin characters (characters with the same syllable pronunciation, including tone) represented by a single homographic component are given in alphabetical order in pinyin. Characters and their syllable pronunciations are taken from Xinhua Zidian (1971).

Providing information about the graph-sound correspondence in Mandarin may serve to help the student of Chinese to recognize some of the regularity inherent in the Chinese writing system. Teachers of Chinese may also find this book useful in seeing how characters and character components may be organized in Mandarin.

huí

回(huí)
茴(huí)
洄(huí)
蛔(huí)

jiōng

扃(jiōng)
坰(jiōng)

kāng

康(kāng)
糠(kāng)
慷(kāng)
槺(kāng)

kàng

亢(kàng)
抗(kàng)
炕(kàng)
钪(kàng)
伉(kàng)

kǎo

考(kǎo)

烤(kǎo)

拷(kǎo)

栲(kǎo)

kōng

空(kōng)
箜(kōng)
崆(kōng)

kòng

空(kòng)
控(kòng)

kōu

眍(kōu)
抠(kōu)

kuān

宽(kuān)

髋(kuān)

kuāng

匡(kuāng)
框(kuāng)
筐(kuāng)
洭(kuāng)
哐(kuāng)
诓(kuāng)

kuáng

狂(kuáng)
诳(kuáng)

lái

来(lái)

莱(lái)

錸(lái)

涞(lái)

徕(lái)

崃(lái)

liǎng

两(liǎng)
俩(liǎng)
魉(liǎng)
唡(liǎng)

liě

两(liǎng)
俩(liǎng)
魉(liǎng)
唡(liǎng)

liě

咧(liě)
裂(liě)

lǐn

凛(lǐn)
廪(lǐn)
檩(lǐn)
懔(lǐn)

lǐng

令(lǐng)
领(lǐng)
岭(lǐng)

liū

溜(liū)
熘(liū)

lǒng

笼(lǒng)

陇(lǒng)

拢(lǒng)

垄(lǒng)

lòng

弄(lòng)
衖(lòng)

lōu

摟(lōu)
瞜(lōu)

lǒu

搂(lǒu)
篓(lǒu)
嵝(lǒu)

mǎ

马(mǎ)
吗(mǎ)
蚂(mǎ)
犸(mǎ)
玛(mǎ)
码(mǎ)

mǎn

满(mǎn)
蟎(mǎn)

màn

曼(màn)
慢(màn)
漫(màn)
蔓(màn)
墁(màn)
幔(màn)
缦(màn)
谩(màn)
镘(màn)
熳(màn)

mǎng

莽(mǎng)
蟒(mǎng)

References

Handian [<汉典>, ‘字典’]. Online Chinese dictionary. (2004 – 2015). http://www.zdic.net

Kraemer, Stephen M.(2021g). *Homographic Components in Homophonous Mandarin Characters*. Independent Publishing Platform.

Xinhua zidian (New China dictionary). (1971). Beijing: Shangwu Yinshuguan. [<新华字典>, 1971, 北京：商务印书馆.]

Zhou, Youguang. (1980). *Hanzi shengpang duyin biancha* (A handy look up for the pronunciation of phonetics in Chinese characters). Jilin: Jilin Remnin Chubanshe.
[周 有光, 1980, <汉字声旁读音便查>，吉林：吉林人民出版社.]

Books on the Chinese Writing System by Stephen M. Kraemer

Available on Amazon.com

(www.amazon.com/author/stephenkraemer)

Kraemer, Stephen M. (2017a). *Let's Learn Mandarin Phonics. Seven Basic Phonetic Patterns of Commonly Occurring Chinese Characters.* CreateSpace Independent Publishing Platform.

Kraemer, Stephen M. (2017b). *Let's Learn Mandarin Phonics-2. Final and Final-Tone Perfect Phonetic Patterns of Common Chinese Characters.* CreateSpace Independent Publishing Platform.

Kraemer, Stephen M. (2018a). *Let's Learn Mandarin Phonics-3. Rime Clue, Rime-Tone Clue, Ending Clue, Ending-Tone Clue Phonetic Patterns of Common Chinese Characters.* CreateSpace Independent Publishing Platform.

Kraemer, Stephen M. (2018b). *Let's Learn Mandarin Phonics-4. Initial Clue, Initial-Tone Clue, Tone-Clue and Related Phonetic Patterns of Common Chinese Characters.* CreateSpace Independent Publishing Platform.

Kraemer, Stephen M. (2018c). *Let's Learn Mandarin Phonics-5. Vowel Phonetic Clues for Common Chinese Characters.* CreateSpace Independent Publishing Platform.

Kraemer, Stephen M. (2018d). *Phonetic Clues for Learning Common Chinese Characters.* CreateSpace Independent Publishing Platform.

Kraemer, Stephen M. (2018e). *A Phonetic Guide to Learning Chinese Characters*. CreateSpace Independent Publishing Platform.

Kraemer, Stephen M. (2018f). *Let's Learn Pinyin Final "i" Chinese Characters in Mandarin*. CreateSpace Independent Publishing Platform.

Kraemer, Stephen M. (2018g). *Homorganic Initial Patterns in Common Mandarin Chinese Characters*. CreateSpace Independent Publishing Platform.

Kraemer, Stephen M. (2018h). *Let's Learn Pinyin Final "u/ü" Patterns in Mandarin Chinese Characters*. CreateSpace Independent Publishing Platform.

Kraemer, Stephen M. (2018i). *Coronal Initial Patterns in Common Mandarin Chinese Characters*. CreateSpace Independent Publishing Platform.

Kraemer, Stephen M. (2018j). *Voiceless Alveolar/Retroflex Initial Patterns in Mandarin Chinese Characters*. CreateSpace Independent Publishing Platform.

Kraemer, Stephen M. (2018k). *Velar/Palatal Initial Patterns in Mandarin Chinese Characters*. CreateSpace Independent Publishing Platform.

Kraemer, Stephen M. (2018l). *Pinyin 'an' Rime Patterns in Mandarin Chinese Characters*. CreateSpace Independent Publishing Platform.

Kraemer, Stephen M. (2018m). *Let's Learn Pinyin "n/ng" Ending Patterns in Mandarin Chinese Characters.* CreateSpace Independent Publishing Platform.

Kraemer, Stephen M. (2018n). *Final Patterns in Pinyin "ng" Ending Mandarin Chinese Characters.* CreateSpace Independent Publishing Platform.

Kraemer, Stephen M. (2019). *Initial Perfect and Initial-Tone Perfect Patterns in Mandarin Chinese Characters.* Independent Publishing Platform.

Kraemer, Stephen M. (2019a). *Initial-Rime Perfect and Initial-Ending Perfect Patterns in Mandarin Chinese Characters.* Independent Publishing Platform.

Kraemer, Stephen M. (2019b). *Similar Vowel Patterns in Initial-Perfect Mandarin Chinese Characters.* Independent Publishing Platform.

Kraemer, Stephen M. (2019c). *Homorganic Variation in the Pronunciation of Chinese Characters in Mandarin.* Independent Publishing Platform.

Kraemer, Stephen M. (2019d). *Coronal Variation in the Pronunciation of Chinese Characters in Mandarin.* Independent Publishing Platform.

Kraemer, Stephen M. (2019e). *Pronunciation Variation in V and VC1 Segment Characters in Mandarin.* Independent Publishing Platform.

Kraemer, Stephen M. (2019f). *Dorsal/Coronal Variation in the Pronunciation of Chinese Characters in Mandarin*. Independent Publishing Platform.

Kraemer, Stephen M. (2019g). *A Phonetic Guide to Mandarin Chinese Characters in Color*. Independent Publishing Platform.

Kraemer, Stephen M. (2019h). *Phonetic Clues for Mandarin Chinese Characters in Color*. Independent Publishing Platform.

Kraemer, Stephen M. (2019i). *More Phonetic Clues for Mandarin Chinese Characters in Color*. Independent Publishing Platform.

Kraemer, Stephen M. (2019j). *Even More Phonetic Clues for Mandarin Chinese Characters in Color*. Independent Publishing Platform.

Kraemer, Stephen M. (2019k). *Phonetic Patterns in Mandarin Chinese Characters*. Independent Publishing Platform.

Kraemer, Stephen M. (2019l). *More Phonetic Patterns in Mandarin Chinese Characters*. Independent Publishing Platform.

Kraemer, Stephen M. (2019m). *Even More Phonetic Patterns in Mandarin Chinese Characters*. Independent Publishing Platform.

Kraemer, Stephen M. (2019n). *Still More Phonetic Clues for Mandarin Chinese Characters in Color*. Independent Publishing Platform.

Kraemer, Stephen M. (2019o). *More and More Phonetic Clues for Mandarin Chinese Characters in Color*. Independent Publishing Platform.

Kraemer, Stephen M. (2019p). *Still More Phonetic Patterns in Mandarin Chinese Characters*. Independent Publishing Platform.

Kraemer, Stephen M. (2019q). *A Phonetic Color Guide to Mandarin Chinese Characters*. Independent Publishing Platform.

Kraemer, Stephen M. (2019r).
Pinyin "ch/c" Initial Patterns in Mandarin Chinese Characters. Independent Publishing Platform.

Kraemer, Stephen M. (2019s).
Pinyin "zh/z" Initial Patterns in Mandarin Chinese Characters. Independent Publishing Platform.

Kraemer, Stephen M. (2019t).
Pinyin "sh/s" Initial Patterns in Mandarin Chinese Characters. Independent Publishing Platform.

Kraemer, Stephen M. (2019u).
Pinyin "sh/x" Initial Patterns in Mandarin Chinese Characters. Independent Publishing Platform.

Kraemer, Stephen M. (2019v). *Pinyin "zh/j" Initial Patterns in Mandarin Chinese Characters*. Independent Publishing Platform.

Kraemer, Stephen M. (2019w). *Pinyin "z/c" Initial Patterns in Mandarin Chinese Characters*. Independent Publishing Platform.

Kraemer, Stephen M. (2019x). *Dental Initial Patterns in Mandarin Chinese Characters*. Independent Publishing Platform.

Kraemer, Stephen M. (2019y). *Dental/Palatal Initial Patterns in Mandarin Chinese Characters*. Independent Publishing Platform.

Kraemer, Stephen M. (2019z). *Retroflex/Palatal Initial Patterns in Mandarin Chinese Characters*. Independent Publishing Platform.

Kraemer, Stephen M. (2019aa). *Final Patterns in Velar/Palatal Mandarin Chinese Characters*. Independent Publishing Platform.

Kraemer, Stephen M. (2019ab). *Pinyin "e/i" Single Vowel Patterns in Mandarin Chinese Characters*. Independent Publishing Platform.

Kraemer, Stephen M. (2019ac). *Pinyin "a/e" Single Vowel Patterns in Mandarin Chinese Characters*. Independent Publishing Platform.

Kraemer, Stephen M. (2019ad). *Retroflex/Dental Initial Patterns in Mandarin Chinese Characters*. Independent Publishing Platform.

Kraemer, Stephen M. (2019ae). *Pinyin "ch/sh" Initial Patterns in Mandarin Chinese Characters*. Independent Publishing Platform.

Kraemer, Stephen M. (2019af). *Pinyin "zh/sh" Initial Patterns in Mandarin Chinese Characters*. Independent Publishing Platform.

Kraemer, Stephen M. (2019ag). *Pinyin "zh/ch" Initial Patterns in Mandarin Chinese Characters*. Independent Publishing Platform.

Kraemer, Stephen M. (2019ah). *Retroflex Initial Patterns in Mandarin Chinese Characters*. Independent Publishing Platform.

Kraemer, Stephen M. (2019ai). *Palatal/ "l" Initial Patterns in Mandarin Chinese Characters*. Independent Publishing Platform.

Kraemer, Stephen M. (2019aj). *Alveolar/Palatal Initial Patterns in Mandarin Chinese Characters*. Independent Publishing Platform.

Kraemer, Stephen M. (2019ak). *Retroflex/Voiced Alveolar Initial Patterns in Mandarin Chinese Characters*. Independent Publishing Platform.

Kraemer, Stephen M. (2019al). *Pinyin "y" Patterns in Mandarin Chinese Characters*. Independent Publishing Platform.

Kraemer, Stephen M. (2019am). *Pinyin "w" and "w/y" Patterns in Mandarin Chinese Characters*. Independent Publishing Platform.

Kraemer, Stephen M. (2019an). *V Segment Patterns in Mandarin Chinese Characters*. Independent Publishing Platform.

Kraemer, Stephen M. (2019ao). *Pinyin "ai/i" Vowel Patterns in Mandarin Chinese Characters*. Independent Publishing Platform.

Kraemer, Stephen M. (2019ap). *Phonetic Patterns in Mandarin Chinese Characters: Pinyin "a" Finals and Unrounded Diphthongs*. Independent Publishing Platform.

Kraemer, Stephen M. (2019aq). *Phonetic Patterns in Mandarin Chinese Characters: Pinyin "e" Finals and Unrounded Diphthongs*. Independent Publishing Platform.

Kraemer, Stephen M. (2019ar). *Phonetic Patterns in Mandarin Chinese Characters: Unrounded Diphthong Finals*. Independent Publishing Platform.

Kraemer, Stephen M. (2019as). *Phonetic Patterns in Mandarin Chinese Characters: Rounded Medial Vowels in V Finals*. Independent Publishing Platform.

Kraemer, Stephen M. (2019at). *Phonetic Patterns in Mandarin Chinese Characters: Rounded Medial and Rounded Ending Vowels in V Finals*. Independent Publishing Platform.

Kraemer, Stephen M. (2019au). *Phonetic Patterns in Mandarin Chinese Characters: Pinyin "u" and Rounded Medial Vowels in V Finals*. Independent Publishing Platform.

Kraemer, Stephen M. (2019av). *Phonetic Patterns of Chinese Characters: Velar / "w" and Velar / "y" in Mandarin*. Independent Publishing Platform.

Kraemer, Stephen M. (2019aw). *Phonetic Patterns of Chinese Characters: Alveolar / "y" in Mandarin*. Independent Publishing Platform.

Kraemer, Stephen M. (2019ax). *Phonetic Patterns of Chinese Characters: Retroflex / "y" in Mandarin*. Independent Publishing Platform.

Kraemer, Stephen M. (2019ay). *Phonetic Patterns of Chinese Characters: Palatal / "y" in Mandarin*. Independent Publishing Platform.

Kraemer, Stephen M. (2019az). *Phonetic Patterns of Chinese Characters: Pinyin "g/k" in Mandarin*. Independent Publishing Platform.

Kraemer, Stephen M. (2019aaa). *Phonetic Patterns of Chinese Characters: Pinyin "g/h" in Mandarin*. Independent Publishing Platform.

Kraemer, Stephen M. (2019aab). *Phonetic Patterns of Chinese Characters: Pinyin "h/k" in Mandarin*. Independent Publishing Platform.

Kraemer, Stephen M. (2019aac). *Phonetic Patterns of Chinese Characters: Velar Initials in Mandarin*. Independent Publishing Platform.

Kraemer, Stephen M. (2019aad). *Phonetic Patterns in Mandarin Chinese Characters: Pinyin "i/ie" Finals*. Independent Publishing Platform.

Kraemer, Stephen M. (2019aae). *Phonetic Patterns in Mandarin Chinese Characters: Pinyin "i/a" and "i/ei" Finals*. Independent Publishing Platform.

Kraemer, Stephen M. (2019aaf). *Phonetic Patterns of Chinese Characters: Pinyin "d/t" Initials in Mandarin*. Independent Publishing Platform.

Kraemer, Stephen M. (2019aag). *Phonetic Patterns of Chinese Characters: Alveolar Initials in Mandarin*. Independent Publishing Platform.

Kraemer, Stephen M. (2019aah). *Phonetic Patterns of Chinese Characters: Pinyin "b/p" Initials in Mandarin*. Independent Publishing Platform.

Kraemer, Stephen M. (2019aai). *Phonetic Patterns of Chinese Characters: Pinyin "f/b" and "f/p" Initials in Mandarin*. Independent Publishing Platform.

Kraemer, Stephen M. (2019aaj). *Phonetic Patterns of Chinese Characters: Labial Initials in Mandarin*. Independent Publishing Platform.

Kraemer, Stephen M. (2019aak). *Phonetic Patterns in Mandarin Chinese Characters: Pinyin "uo" and Unrounded V Finals*. Independent Publishing Platform.

Kraemer, Stephen M. (2019aal). *Phonetic Patterns in Mandarin Chinese Characters: Pinyin "u" and Unrounded V Finals*. Independent Publishing Platform.

Kraemer, Stephen M.(2019aam). *Phonetic Patterns in Mandarin Chinese Characters: Pinyin "u" and Rounded Ending Vowels in V Finals*. Independent Publishing Platform.

Kraemer, Stephen M.(2019aan). *Phonetic Patterns in Mandarin Chinese Characters: Rounded Ending Vowels in V Finals*. Independent Publishing Platform.

Kraemer, Stephen M.(2019aao). *Phonetic Patterns in Mandarin Chinese Characters: Pinyin "an"/"en"/"in" Finals*. Independent Publishing Platform.

Kraemer, Stephen M.(2019aap). *Phonetic Patterns in Mandarin Chinese Characters: V/VC1 Finals with a Rounded Vowel*. Independent Publishing Platform.

Kraemer, Stephen M.(2019aaq). *Phonetic Patterns in Mandarin Chinese Characters: V Finals with a Rounded Vowel Plus VC1 Finals with Unrounded V*. Independent Publishing Platform.

Kraemer, Stephen M.(2019aar). *Phonetic Patterns in Mandarin Chinese Characters: V/VC1 Finals with Unrounded Vowels*. Independent Publishing Platform.

Kraemer, Stephen M.(2019aas). *Phonetic Patterns in Mandarin Chinese Characters: Pinyin "n" Ending Finals with One Rounded Vowel*. Independent Publishing Platform.

Kraemer, Stephen M.(2019aat). *Phonetic Patterns in Mandarin Chinese Characters: VC1 Finals with One Rounded Vowel*. Independent Publishing Platform.

Kraemer, Stephen M.(2019aau). *Phonetic Patterns in Mandarin Chinese Characters: Pinyin "n" Ending Finals with Rounded and Unrounded Vowels*. Independent Publishing Platform.

Kraemer, Stephen M.(2019aav). *Phonetic Patterns in Mandarin Chinese Characters: VC1 Finals with Rounded and Unrounded Vowels*. Independent Publishing Platform.

Kraemer, Stephen M.(2020). *Phonetic Patterns in Mandarin Chinese Characters: Pinyin "ng" Ending Finals with Unrounded Vowels*. Independent Publishing Platform.

Kraemer, Stephen M.(2020a). *Phonetic Patterns in Mandarin Chinese Characters: Pinyin "n/ng" Ending Finals with Unrounded Vowels*. Independent Publishing Platform.

Kraemer, Stephen M.(2020b). *Phonetic Patterns in Mandarin Chinese Characters: V/VC1 Finals*. Independent Publishing Platform.

Kraemer, Stephen M.(2020c). *Phonetic Patterns in Mandarin Chinese Characters: VC1 Finals with Unrounded Vowels*. Independent Publishing Platform.

Kraemer, Stephen M.(2020d). *Phonetic Patterns in Mandarin Chinese Characters: V Finals with a Rounded Medial Vowel Plus Unrounded V*. Independent Publishing Platform.

Kraemer, Stephen M.(2020e). *Phonetic Patterns in Mandarin Chinese Characters: V Finals with a Rounded Ending Vowel Plus Unrounded V*. Independent Publishing Platform.

Kraemer, Stephen M.(2020f). *Phonetic Patterns in Mandarin Chinese Characters: Labial/Velar Initials and Pinyin "m"/ "w"*. Independent Publishing Platform.

Kraemer, Stephen M.(2020g). *Phonetic Patterns in Mandarin Chinese Characters: Velar/Retroflex Initials*. Independent Publishing Platform.

Kraemer, Stephen M.(2020h). *Phonetic Patterns in Mandarin Chinese Characters: Velar/Alveolar Initials*. Independent Publishing Platform.

Kraemer, Stephen M.(2020i). *Phonetic Patterns in Mandarin Chinese Characters: Palatal Initials*. Independent Publishing Platform.

Kraemer, Stephen M.(2020j). *Phonetic Patterns in Chinese Characters: Pinyin "a/e" Variation in Mandarin*. Independent Publishing Platform.

Kraemer, Stephen M.(2020k). *Phonetic Groups in Chinese Characters: All Unrounded Vowel Finals in Mandarin*. Independent Publishing Platform.

Kraemer, Stephen M.(2020l). *Phonetic Groups in Chinese Characters: All Unrounded Vowel Finals in Mandarin Volume 2*. Independent Publishing Platform.

Kraemer, Stephen M.(2020m). *Phonetic Groups in Chinese Characters: All Unrounded Vowel Finals in Mandarin Volume 3*. Independent Publishing Platform.

Kraemer, Stephen M.(2020n). *Phonetic Groups in Chinese Characters: All Vowel Finals in Mandarin*. Independent Publishing Platform.

Kraemer, Stephen M.(2020o). *Phonetic Groups in Chinese Characters: All Vowel Finals in Mandarin Volume 2*. Independent Publishing Platform.

Kraemer, Stephen M.(2020p). *Phonetic Groups in Chinese Characters: All Vowel Finals in Mandarin Volume 3*. Independent Publishing Platform.

Kraemer, Stephen M.(2020q). *Phonetic Patterns in Mandarin Chinese Characters: Final Perfect with Palatal j/x, q/x Initials*. Independent Publishing Platform.

Kraemer, Stephen M.(2020r). *Phonetic Groups in Chinese Characters: All Unrounded Vowel Finals in Mandarin Volume 4*. Independent Publishing Platform.

Kraemer, Stephen M.(2020s). *Phonetic Groups in Chinese Characters: All Vowel Finals in Mandarin Volume 4*. Independent Publishing Platform.

Kraemer, Stephen M.(2020t). *Phonetic Patterns in Mandarin Chinese Characters: Final Perfect with Palatal j/q Initials*. Independent Publishing Platform.

Kraemer, Stephen M.(2020u). *Phonetic Patterns in Mandarin Chinese Characters: Final Perfect with Palatal Initials*. Independent Publishing Platform.

Kraemer, Stephen M.(2020v). *Phonetic Components for Meaning in Mandarin Chinese Characters*. Independent Publishing Platform.

Kraemer, Stephen M.(2020w). *Phonetic Components for Meaning in Mandarin Chinese Characters Volume 2.* Independent Publishing Platform.

Kraemer, Stephen M.(2020x). *Phonetic Components for Meaning in Mandarin Chinese Characters Volume 3.* Independent Publishing Platform.

Kraemer, Stephen M.(2020y). *Phonetic Components for Meaning in Mandarin Chinese Characters Volume 4.* Independent Publishing Platform.

Kraemer, Stephen M.(2020z). *Phonetic Components for Meaning in Mandarin Chinese Characters Volume 5.* Independent Publishing Platform.

Kraemer, Stephen M.(2020aa). *Phonetic Components for Meaning in Mandarin Chinese Characters Volume 6.* Independent Publishing Platform.

Kraemer, Stephen M.(2020ab). *Phonetic Components for Meaning in Mandarin Chinese Characters Volume 7.* Independent Publishing Platform.

Kraemer, Stephen M.(2020ac). *Semantic Compounds in Mandarin Chinese Characters*. Independent Publishing Platform.

Kraemer, Stephen M.(2020ad). *Patterns and Formulas for Phonetic Groups in Mandarin Chinese Characters*. Independent Publishing Platform.

Kraemer, Stephen M.

(2020ae-ah).
Patterns and Formulas for Phonetic Groups in Mandarin Chinese Characters Volume 2-5. Independent Publishing Platform.

Kraemer, Stephen M.

(2020ai-al).
Patterns and Formulas for Phonetic Groups in Mandarin Chinese Characters Volume 6-9. Independent Publishing Platform.

Kraemer, Stephen M.

(2020am-ap).
Patterns and Formulas for Phonetic Groups in Mandarin Chinese Characters Volume 10-12, 14. Independent Publishing Platform.

Kraemer, Stephen M.
(2020aq-at).
Patterns and Formulas for Phonetic Groups in Mandarin Chinese Characters Volume 15-18.
Independent Publishing Platform.

Kraemer, Stephen M.
(2020au-ax).
Patterns and Formulas for Phonetic Groups in Mandarin Chinese Characters Volume 19-22.
Independent Publishing Platform.

Kraemer, Stephen M.
(2020ay-aab).
Patterns and Formulas for Phonetic Groups in Mandarin Chinese Characters Volume 23-26.
Independent Publishing Platform.

Kraemer, Stephen M.
(2020aac-aaf).
Patterns and Formulas for Phonetic Groups in Mandarin Chinese Characters Volume 27-30.
Independent Publishing Platform.

Kraemer, Stephen M.
(2020aag-aaj).
Patterns and Formulas for Phonetic Groups in Mandarin Chinese Characters Volume 31-34.
Independent Publishing Platform.

Kraemer, Stephen M.
(2020aak-aan).
Patterns and Formulas for Phonetic Groups in Mandarin Chinese Characters Volume 35-38.
Independent Publishing Platform.

Kraemer, Stephen M.

(2020aao-aar).
Patterns and Formulas for Phonetic Groups in Mandarin Chinese Characters Volume 39-42.
Independent Publishing Platform.

Kraemer, Stephen M.

(2020aas-aav).
Patterns and Formulas for Phonetic Groups in Mandarin Chinese Characters Volume 43-46.
Independent Publishing Platform.

Kraemer, Stephen M.

(2020aaw-aaz).
Patterns and Formulas for Phonetic Groups in Mandarin Chinese Characters Volume 47-50.
Independent Publishing Platform.

Kraemer, Stephen M.
(2020aaaa-aaad).
Patterns and Formulas for Phonetic Groups in Mandarin Chinese Characters Volume 51-54.
Independent Publishing Platform.

Kraemer, Stephen M.
(2020aaae-aaah).
Patterns and Formulas for Phonetic Groups in Mandarin Chinese Characters Volume 55-58.
Independent Publishing Platform

Kraemer, Stephen M.(2021).
Patterns and Formulas for Phonetic Groups in Mandarin Chinese Characters Volume 58.
Independent Publishing Platform.

Kraemer, Stephen M.(2021a-d). *Patterns and Formulas for Phonetic Groups in Mandarin Chinese Characters Volume 59-62.* Independent Publishing Platform.

Kraemer, Stephen M.(2021e-f). *Patterns and Formulas for Phonetic Groups in Mandarin Chinese Characters Volume 63-64.* Independent Publishing Platform.

Kraemer, Stephen M.(2021g). *Homographic Components in Homophonous Mandarin Characters*. Independent Publishing Platform.

www.ingramcontent.com/pod-product-compliance
Lightning Source LLC
LaVergne TN
LVHW010454160826
845677LV00012B/2482

* 9 7 9 8 7 0 6 1 3 2 4 9 1 *